A 30-DAY JOURNEY
OF INSPIRATION, FAITH, AND ACTION

Now's the Time!

OUTREACH®

Now's the Time

© 2016 by Outreach, Inc.

Published by Outreach, Inc., Colorado Springs, CO 80919

www.Outreach.com

ISBN: 9781635100389

Cover Design by Tim Downs
Interior Design by Alexia Garaventa
Written by Jeremy Jones
Edited by Tia Smith

Printed in the United States of America

To:

_____

From:

_____

CONTENTS

TIME FOR CONNECTION

TIME FOR COMPASSION

INTRODUCTION

We hope that this book is a next step in your journey of faith. As you read and reflect on each of the thirty devotions, may God continue to draw you closer to His heart and fill you with hope, grace, connection, and compassion.

This book is also an invitation to continue exploring church and your place in our community. We believe church is so much more than the four walls of a building. As a church, we are a body, a group of people who come together to collectively turn our attention toward God and remember Whose we are. We join to worship our God and to be transformed by Him. We share our hopes together. We extend grace to one another as God has extended grace to each of us. We connect with each other in our joys and pains, our highs and lows, our hard times and blessings. And we offer compassion to each other and to the world around us as living reminders of the love and forgiveness offered to us all in Christ.

This book can be read alone, with a partner, or as part of a small-group study. However you read it, and wherever you are on your spiritual journey, this book can be a guide to the next steps in your relationship with God. Let Him be your true guide as you take time to reflect on Scripture and to write down your own thoughts, prayers, struggles, and victories. Will you allow God to fill you and lead you deeper into His story?

Jump in. Get started today. As 2 Corinthians 6:2 tells us, "Now is the time of God's favor, now is the day of salvation." Don't let today pass you by.

IT'S TIME

Yet a time is coming and has now come
when the true worshipers will worship the Father
in the Spirit and in truth, for they are the kind
of worshipers the Father seeks.

(John 4:23)

THERE IS AN OLD SUMMER camp skit where a line of people sit in chairs with their legs crossed on an empty stage. At various intervals, the last person in line asks the next person, "Is it time?" The question gets passed from person to person until it reaches the first person, who looks at her watch and answers, "No, not yet." This goes on and on until finally the first person's reply changes to "It's time!" At this point everyone switches which leg is crossed and goes back to staring blankly ahead. The skit is funny at best, depressing at worst. But it reflects how easily we allow the schedules and constraints of our world to dictate what we do and when we do it—and we often find that we are consumed with the unimportant.

Now is the time for that to change. It's time for more. God wants to redeem our time—our past, present, and future. He wants to infuse the eternal into our limited time on earth. And He wants to start today. John 4:23 says that the time has come when the Father is looking for those who will worship, not based on rules, regulations, or obligations, but in the Spirit and in truth.

How do we do that? Through thoughtful study of Scripture, in conversation with God through prayer, and by simply abiding in Him. Throw off the temptation to just keep going and instead take the time to rest in Him, worship Him for who He is, and allow Him to bring more hope, grace, connection, and compassion into your life.

What time is it in your life? What is it time for? Will you open your heart and allow God to fill you and lead you deeper into relationship with Him?

Time for
HOPE

SECURE HOPE

*We have this hope as an anchor
for the soul, firm and secure.*

(Hebrews 6:19)

THE WIND IS HOWLING; THE waves are crashing. Heavy rain pelts down, and water surges all around. A boat caught in bad weather depends on its anchor for survival. While we often think an anchor is just used to keep a boat in one place, that only happens in calm waters. An anchor isn't actually tied onto anything; it merely holds a boat in a general area by preventing it from drifting too far. But perhaps more importantly, an anchor is used to stabilize a boat in inclement weather. The heavy object creates drag through the water, slowing the boat down. The anchor can also prevent a boat from turning sideways to the waves and being overwhelmed by them. Rather than something that weighs a boat down or holds it back, the anchor provides protection in the worst situations and increases control. For anyone caught on a boat in a storm, a good anchor is vital.

The writer of Hebrews tells us that our hope in God is our anchor in life, and it's a good anchor—firm and secure. We often think of hope in different terms. Our ordinary use of *hope* implies uncertainty—we hope for something that may or may not happen. Or we hope for something we desire but that seems out of reach. But our hope in the Lord is just the opposite. Biblical hope is a confident expectation, a sure desire. Like an anchor, it provides protection when the storms of life come and the waves rise. Our hope is in the One who controls the waves. He is unchanging and all-powerful.

He is mighty yet loves each of us. We can hold tight and place our hope in Him, knowing He will anchor us in the storm.

What in your life feels firm and secure? What do you hope in and for? How does seeing hope in God as firm and secure change the way you trust and obey Him?

HOPE IN UNFAILING LOVE

*The L*ORD *delights in those who fear him,*
who put their hope in his unfailing love.

(Psalm 147:11)

IN 2012, FILMMAKER JAMES CAMERON became the first person to solo dive to the deepest part of the ocean, the Mariana Trench's Challenger Deep, as part of his documentary *Deepsea Challenge 3D*. Going 6.8 miles deep in his submarine, Cameron took pictures, gathered scientific data, and saw with his own eyes what no one has seen since a 1960 expedition took the deep dive. And then he had to get back to the surface.

The design of the submarine depended heavily on weights that would carry the ship down to the depths and then release when the pilot was ready to come back up. Those weights dropping were vital to the mission. They could not fail. Cameron's only hope of seeing daylight after his record-breaking dive rested on those weights. And so he and his team tried them time and again. They were tested over and over. Placing hope in something unreliable at 6.8 miles under the ocean would mean certain death.

What is our hope in? When we find ourselves under pressure, what do we depend on? It needs to be something secure and unfailing, and the Bible tells us the only sure thing is God's love. Technically, even something as tested and reliable as Cameron's weight system *could* have failed. But God's love does not. His love never fails.

God's love is stronger and more powerful than any other force in or beyond the universe. That's where fear comes in. It seems almost strange to our ears to hear that God delights in those who fear Him. But the delight comes because those who fear God do not fear the world. The world is not our ultimate threat because God is even more powerful. When we recognize that, we can place ourselves in that tension between the fear of the Lord and His unfailing love that casts out all fear. God delights in those who recognize who He is and put their trust in Him. And we have hope in His unfailing love because nothing in the world can overcome it.

What do you fear? How can recognizing the power of God's unfailing love help you to place your hope in Him?

FROM SUFFERING TO HOPE

And we boast in the hope of the glory of God. Not only so, but we also glory in our sufferings, because we know that suffering produces perseverance; perseverance, character; and character, hope. And hope does not put us to shame, because God's love has been poured out into our hearts through the Holy Spirit, who has been given to us.

(Romans 5:2–5)

HAVE YOU EVER BEEN LOST? Have you ever found yourself driving in a new city or hiking through the woods and had that nagging feeling that you just aren't going the right way? You may be following the landmarks or the directions someone gave you, and your map says you're on track—but it just doesn't feel quite right. Things aren't as you expected.

This passage can feel a little bit that way. In our spiritual journeys, we want hope. Hope is, well, hopeful. But the way to get there can often feel wrong. It seems like hope should feel good— like encouragement and victory. But hope is counterintuitive. First we suffer, then we must persevere in that suffering. That builds character in us, and out of that comes hope. It's not such a feel-good process. But the beauty comes at the end of verse 5. It's like that moment when you turn the corner and suddenly your destination is before you. Nothing felt quite right along the way, but you have made it. Hope doesn't put us to shame because it is based on God's unfailing love poured into our hearts. That is why way back at the point of suffering, we can "glory" or rejoice in our suffering. Because we know that even when we feel lost, we are headed straight for hope.

What suffering are you experiencing right now? Can you see the destination of hope? How does the assurance that you are headed in the right direction help in the tough moments of today?

OVERFLOWING WITH HOPE

May the God of hope fill you with all joy and peace as you trust in him, so that you may overflow with hope by the power of the Holy Spirit.

(Romans 15:13)

NOTHING SAYS SUMMER LIKE A backyard wading pool. Put the hose in, fill it to the top with freezing cold water, and you have hours of endless summer fun for kids, adults, even dogs. But filling the pool can seem to take forever. Even with the hose on full blast, it feels slow. For most of the process, the filling of the pool is hardly even noticeable. But when the water reaches the top rim and starts to spill over the sides, you see more clearly just how much water is flowing. Suddenly it's overflowing and hard to stop. The overflow quickly floods everything around the pool.

This is a picture of God's hope in our lives. Sometimes we don't feel it. Sometimes it is hard to see that God is even working or filling us—the process is slow. But He doesn't stop there. God's desire is that we overflow with hope by the power of the Holy Spirit. He wants the flow of His peace and hope in our lives to become visibly unstoppable. Why? First, because He loves us and wants us to know His abundant love. But it doesn't stop there. God wants the overflow of hope in our lives to flood the people around us. He wants our excess to spread to everyone and everything we encounter so that even more of our world will know the hope, joy, and peace that come from knowing Jesus Christ.

Where in your life do you feel like the filling is slow? Where in your life do you see the over-flowing flood impacting others? How can you use that overflow of hope to deepen your relationship with God and point others to Him?

JOYFUL HOPE

Be joyful in hope, patient in affliction, faithful in prayer.
(Romans 12:12)

ROCK, PAPER, SCISSORS. BACON, LETTUCE, to-
mato. Faith, hope, love. There are lots of things
that go together in threes. While each one of the
three is a separate thing, they fit together into
a perfect trio. So much so that we can't think of
one without the others—the balance would be
off and the triangle incomplete.

Romans 12 contains a perfect trio of principles
for the Christian to live by: "Be joyful in hope, patient in affliction, faithful in prayer." They go together—but unlike BLTs, we often prefer to separate these from each other and just take the one

we like best. We prefer to take the joyful hope without the patient affliction or faithful prayer. But the truth is, as we walk through life, the three are not separate. They are all part of our journeys here on earth. In this world there will always be affliction right alongside joy. And both the joy and the affliction mean we need to stay in communication with God. They are a trio in the lives of Christ followers, and we should let each in turn remind us of the importance of the others.

Where in your life do you see each of these parts of the trio? How can your relationship with God be strengthened by embracing all three?

WAIT IN HOPE

We wait in hope for the L<small>ORD</small>;
he is our help and our shield.

(Psalm 33:20)

PICTURE THE HIGHEST, ROCKIEST MOUNTAIN cliff you've seen. Now imagine yourself as a climber, stranded there. Sheer drop-offs on all sides, crumbling and unstable rock all around. Now imagine two different scenarios. In the first, you realize that nobody knows where you are. There is no way to contact anyone for rescue. There is a desperate franticness to your waiting. But change the scenario with one detail—you know that rescue is on its way. The mountain is still high, the cliffs are still sheer, your position is still risky. But the hope you feel knowing rescue is coming changes everything, even before they arrive.

Romans 8:24–25 says, "For in this hope we were saved. But hope that is seen is no hope at all. Who hopes for what they already have? But if we hope for what we do not yet have, we wait for it patiently."

The way hope of rescue changes the mountain scene is also true in our daily lives. When our circumstances are overwhelming, when we are in desperate need of physical, emotional, intellectual, or spiritual rescue, hope in God as our help and shield changes everything. Confident hope encourages patience because we are not questioning *if* but simply *when*.

Are there areas of life where you feel like the climber stranded on the cliff? How are you waiting? How can hope in God's help bring patience?

PLANS FOR HOPE

"For I know the plans I have for you," declares the Lord,
"plans to prosper you and not to harm you,
plans to give you hope and a future."

(Jeremiah 29:11)

THE LAST ONE OF DR. SEUSS'S books published during his lifetime is called *Oh, the Places You'll Go!* Perhaps you've heard it read at a graduation or been given the book as a going-away gift. Like much of Dr. Seuss's work, it is profound despite its simple singsong style. Phrases like these stick with you:

> You're off to Great Places!
>
> Today is your day!
>
> Your mountain is waiting.

So get on your way!

And will you succeed?

Yes! You will, indeed!
(98 and ¾ percent guaranteed).[1]

In a similar way, this verse from Jeremiah is often read or given to young people embarking on a new stage of life. People on the brink of adventure and discovery, not sure what life holds; people trying to make plans but unsure of what they should be as their entire future lies ahead of them. But while both of these men wrote about the journey of life, this verse in Jeremiah offers so much more—it is so much broader and deeper.

God does not have just one adventure, one plan—but many plans, good plans. These plans

1. Dr. Seuss, *Oh, the Places You'll Go!* (New York: Random House Children's Books, 1960), 44, 42.

are not simply about what job we will get, who we will be in relationship with, or where we will live. God's plans are about our hearts—who we are becoming and who God is revealing Himself to be in our lives. Our journeys aren't 98 and ¾ percent guaranteed, they are 100 percent guaranteed because they rest in the hands of the all-powerful God of the universe. That doesn't mean we are guaranteed great wealth and perfect health. It means that God promises He is in control and He is our hope and our future—both on earth and eternally.

Do you find yourself more focused on the immediate journey or the eternal one? How can knowing that God has good plans for you help as you make decisions each day? What encouragement do you feel from this promise?

Time for
GRACE

SAVED BY GRACE

*For it is by grace you have been saved,
through faith—and this is not from yourselves,
it is the gift of God—not by works,
so that no one can boast.*

(Ephesians 2:8–9)

ISN'T FREE STUFF GREAT? FREE samples in the grocery store. Free bags of goodies at a conference. Free T-shirts at a race or outdoor event. And yet, free quickly becomes hard for us to accept in our success-driven society. Even more than free stuff, we like things that we've earned. We like things that make a statement to others about the great things we've done to get what we have. We like to look good to others, and we like to boast about what we did to get there. And it's especially great if whatever we get makes it look like we are even better than we really are.

Grace puts an abrupt halt to that kind of thinking and motivation. Paul tells us in Ephesians that we were saved by grace through faith. Really, it had nothing to do with us. It's all about God. A free gift that none of us deserves. The passage goes on to say, "not by works, so that no one can boast." Really? Can't we boast a little that we were good enough to make it to church and humble enough to surrender our lives to Christ? Nope—no boasting. This one is all God, and it is a free gift from Him.

In what areas of your life are you tempted to boast and even make yourself seem better than you really are? Take some time to surrender those things to God and thank Him for the gift of being saved by grace.

GRACE THROUGH JESUS

Out of his fullness we have all received grace in place of grace already given. For the law was given through Moses; grace and truth came through Jesus Christ.

(John 1:16–17)

WHILE WE OFTEN POINT TO the moment of salvation as the moment of grace, in reality grace is not a one-time gift. It is the gift that keeps on giving. A limitless flow of grace is continually being given from God. It's as if someone were to give you flowers one day for no reason. What a gift! Unexpected and undeserved. But then imagine that every day after that for the rest of your life, a flower delivery person appeared on your doorstep. Your one-time gift has now become an ongoing and limitless flow. Grace.

That is the grace God has always been about. People often think of God in the Old Testament as a God of judgment. And while the gift of salvation for all through Jesus had not yet been given, God was constantly showing grace to His people. Even the giving of the law was an act of grace—a way for people to make their sin right before a holy God. So grace given through Jesus was not a sudden change for God. Instead, it was a continuation of the grace He had already shown from the beginning of the world. "We have all received grace in place of grace already given," says John. The undeserved gift of salvation through Jesus was grace in place of grace—the next scene in God's unfolding story of love and redemption for the world.

How does seeing grace as an unending flow change the way you see God? Have you accepted God's gift of grace and truth in Jesus Christ?

CONFIDENT IN GRACE

Let us then approach God's throne of grace with confidence, so that we may receive mercy and find grace to help us in our time of need.

(Hebrews 4:16)

THE WIDE, HEAVY DOORS SWING open, gold and shining in the sunlight. In the vast room before you is an ornate throne covered in jewels. A thick scarlet carpet stretches out from before the throne to the place where you stand. You shouldn't be here. Out of respect, you bow low, hoping the royal one on the throne will accept your presence. Throughout much of history, if you found yourself in this position, your life would literally be on the line. In the time of Esther in the Old Testament, even a king's wife could be sentenced to death for showing up in the throne room without a specific invitation. Unless the ruler extended his scepter to you to signal mercy, you would be put to death for entering the throne room uninvited.

But the author of Hebrews tells us that God's throne room is not like those of other rulers. Instead, it is called the "throne of grace," and we are told to approach "with confidence." Our confidence is certainly not in ourselves or anything we've done, but it's because of God's grace. He chooses to extend mercy to us and welcome us into His presence—in fact, His grace is the very thing that allows us not to be consumed by our holy God. His throne room is not a place of fear and death but of joy and delight. It is where we can go to receive mercy and help in our time of need. Come—He invites you in, and grace makes the way.

> Do you feel confident coming into God's presence? What issues or circumstances in your life do you need to bring to His throne and receive His mercy and help in your time of need?

GRACE AND SALT

*Let your conversation be always full of grace,
seasoned with salt, so that you may
know how to answer everyone.*

(Colossians 4:6)

WE LIVE IN AN INCREASINGLY small world. People in places we didn't even know existed a few centuries ago can speak to and see each other in real time via technology. We can travel in hours to places that would have taken a lifetime commitment for our great grandparents to reach. And because of the ease with which we are all connected, our global society is one where ideas and religions and cultures interact daily, in person and through technology. So how do we respond? How can those who believe in Jesus approach these amazing opportunities to interact with people around the world?

In the book of Colossians, Paul gives us a simple recipe to follow as we talk with others. It's the same recipe that worked in a very different world a couple thousand years ago, and it still works today. It's like Great Uncle Adam's secret family recipe, passed down through the generations. But Paul's recipe is for good conversation: full of grace, seasoned with salt. That's it! That's the secret sauce. Seems simple enough, but it's far from basic or easy. Grace allows us to extend the character of God to others as we show them kindness, compassion, and love. Just as God has given His grace freely to us, we give the same to others. Seasoned with salt makes sure we're not watered down and bland, mixed with everyone else and impossible to distinguish. God wants the world to know we belong to Him. He wants His message of love and forgiveness to be clear and distinct as we share it with others. As you engage the world around you in meaningful conversation, let them taste the goodness and grace of God.

Who do you know whose conversation follows this recipe? How can you make your interactions with others full of grace and seasoned with salt?

GRACE AND ETERNAL LIFE

The law was brought in so that the trespass might increase. But where sin increased, grace increased all the more, so that, just as sin reigned in death, so also grace might reign through righteousness to bring eternal life through Jesus Christ our Lord.

(Romans 5:20–21)

DYNAMICS HELP TELL THE STORY of music. A melody played softly and smoothly can communicate an entirely different emotion from the same melody played loudly and choppily. The dynamics communicate feeling and create emotion in the listener. A great symphony can use a steady crescendo, gradually increasing the volume of their song, to build dramatic tension until the piece reaches a climax.

The story of God's love throughout history is like a great musical crescendo. The story starts with God's grace in creation, builds through the grace of the law given to sinners as a way to come back to relationship with God, and then climaxes in the amazing grace of Jesus's love poured out on the cross to redeem the world. As Paul tells us in Romans, where sin increased, grace increased all the more. The cycle of grace and sin builds with the crescendo of God's story through history until grace wins in the death and resurrection of Jesus Christ. Grace reigns in righteousness to bring eternal life.

Keep listening, the story isn't over yet—the orchestra is still playing. Another crescendo is coming when Jesus will come again and all things in heaven and earth will be made right with God.

Where in your own life do you hear the crescendo of God's grace building? Try writing a simple melody or drawing a pattern you can repeat as a reminder that God is continually pouring out grace upon grace in your life.

GRACE
IS ENOUGH

*But he said to me, "My grace is sufficient for you,
for my power is made perfect in weakness."*

(2 Corinthians 12:9)

THERE IS AN ORNAMENT THAT hangs on a
Christmas tree at a local school. It's not the
most beautiful ornament—in fact, it's a little on
the worn side. But it tells a story we all need
to hear in our lives. This snowman ornament
was made years ago by a student, and every
year it seems something has broken—a piece of
the scarf, an arm or a leg, or even a segment
of the snowman body. But each year, someone

has faithfully used a hot glue gun to put it back together. It certainly doesn't look as perfect as on the day it was made, but that ornament has become so strong! Every weak place has been reinforced with hot glue, and it would take a hurricane-force wind through the school to destroy that snowman now.

That hot glue gun is a bit like God's grace in our lives. When we are broken, His grace heals us and binds up our wounds—and in the end, those places are stronger than they were without Him. His power is made perfect in our weakness. We don't like to be broken, but when we are and we allow God's grace to be enough, He can heal the brokenness of our lives. In those hard moments of life, His strength is made perfect in our weakness.

Where do you feel broken and in need of God's grace? Ask God to allow you to see the places where you are stronger because His power is made perfect in your weakness.

ABUNDANT GRACE

Grace and peace be yours in abundance through the knowledge of God and of Jesus our Lord.

(2 Peter 1:2)

WHAT DOES ABUNDANCE LOOK LIKE? What images come to mind? Perhaps a garden at harvest time, filled with plants that hang heavy under the weight of juicy tomatoes, sweet grapes, or fresh peppers. Maybe you see a field covered in brilliant wildflowers that stretches out toward the horizon. A table set with a feast. A home filled with the love and laughter of friends and family. Or maybe it is a wide-open space with endless room for freedom and exploration. Abundance is simply a very large quantity of something.

But abundance doesn't typically just refer to a bunch of useless stuff. The word also carries a connotation of goodness and value—that the large quantity is a very good thing. And indeed, an abundance of grace and peace is a very good thing. As we walk through our spiritual journeys and know more and more of God, we realize that He is a God of abundance. His love, faithfulness, and goodness know no end. And He gives to His children an abundant measure of grace. Good thing, because we need it. Every single one of us. When we clear our lives of the desire for more stuff, more money, more success and instead focus on a desire to know and experience more of God, we see that He is already pouring Himself out to us in abundant grace.

Time for
CONNECTION

Is there anything hindering your view of God's abundant grace? What can you do today to clear your vision and run with purpose toward God's abundance?

VINE AND BRANCHES

I am the vine; you are the branches.
If you remain in me and I in you, you will bear much fruit;
apart from me you can do nothing.

(John 15:5)

JESUS USED SO MANY COMMON, everyday examples to explain things to His disciples. His description of the vine and the branches is one of these. We may not have personal experience with agriculture, but His disciples certainly did. They knew what He was talking about. So what was He talking about?

The statement that He is the vine and we are the branches is not a power play. But it is a clear statement of how things work. God is the giver of life—branches cannot survive and bear fruit without the water and nutrients provided by the vine, and we cannot live apart from our connection to God. Our body may live for a time, but our spirit needs the constant supply of life-giving elements that comes from God.

Connection to God is vital for our spiritual growth. Without Him we can work incredibly hard to create goodness, gentleness, kindness, and other fruits of the Spirit in our lives. But we are quickly drained, and the evidence of our relationship with Jesus is not there. When we are connected, we can thrive, produce fruit, and grow in and among other branches. Without Him we wither, but connected to Him we begin to grow. Our connection to God must come first. Connection to others is important, but it cannot sustain us if our primary connection is not to God Himself.

Are you thriving or withering? List three ways you can abide more closely with God this week and allow Him to feed and sustain your spirit.

BODY
OF CHRIST

Now you are the body of Christ,
and each one of you is a part of it.

(1 Corinthians 12:27)

HAVE YOU BELIEVED IN JESUS as Savior? Then you are part of the body of Christ. It may seem strange at first to think of ourselves and the believers around us as parts of one body. "Oh look, that guy is definitely a big toe." "Yeah, and she's the left earlobe for sure." Sounds like crazy talk, right? But the body of Christ is an analogy for how we as believers all fit and work together toward one purpose. Like the parts of a body, we are all different and function in very different ways, but each one is necessary for the health and completeness of the body.

When we believe in Jesus and receive salvation through grace, we become part of this community called the body of Christ. It's a wonderful place of belonging and connection. That connection creates natural opportunities to bless and be blessed as each person expresses their unique gifts. But this isn't the local fitness center—the goal is not just a good-looking body. The goal is the unity of every believer using his or her gifts for the shared purpose of the common good. And when the body is healthy with everyone living in unity, Jesus says, "Then the world will know that you [God the Father] sent me and have loved them even as you have loved me" (John 17:23). The world is looking to understand what our God is all about. Do we reflect Him well?

Are you an active part of the body of Christ, or are you looking out only for yourself? How can you be more unified with other believers toward the common goal of showing the world Jesus's love?

BE ONE

*Then make my joy complete
by being like-minded, having the same love,
being one in spirit and of one mind.*

(Philippians 2:2)

HAVE YOU EVER WATCHED SYNCHRONIZED swimming? It's a sport that combines swimming with aspects of dance and gymnastics. In competition, groups of athletes perform a routine in perfect unison. While it may not have the reputation for excitement that comes with the Super Bowl or March Madness, when you take the time to watch, it is fascinating and compelling. The athletes move as if their limbs are attached to each other, or at least controlled by one central mind. So perfect is their timing and so coordinated are their movements, it's hard to imagine how they maintain such unison—especially in water. The unity the athletes show in their routines doesn't come easily. Hard work and long practices are required. But when done well, the result is mesmerizing.

This is how we as believers should appear to the world. They should see in us a unity and like-mindedness that is compelling and hard to explain. Unity is not easy to accomplish, and it requires hard work and practice to come together and learn to be like-minded and have the same love for others. But truly being one in spirit and mind, showing consistent love to the world around us, has the potential to transform us as well as those we encounter.

Do you belong to a group of unified believers? How can you grow in unity with others so the world sees a genuine oneness of mind and spirit?

STRENGTH IN NUMBERS

Though one may be overpowered,
two can defend themselves.
A cord of three strands is not quickly broken.

(Ecclesiastes 4:12)

ROPE MAKING HAS BEEN AROUND throughout recorded history. Whether plants, twine, or plastic, people have been twisting together strands of whatever material they have on hand to make a stronger rope. This is a practical solution to a practical problem. People need to pull, bind, lift, and haul heavy things, and they need strong rope to do it. So they twist together weaker strands to make something strong enough to withhold the pressure of the job. The process of twisting three strands together is relatively simple, and the outcome is a huge improvement in strength and functionality.

This is why the Bible uses a rope or cord of three strands to explain the importance of connection. Many people have studied the Bible and associated this verse from Ecclesiastes with different relationships—the relationship of believers and God, the relationship of a married couple and God. But regardless of the specifics, it is clear that three strands are exponentially stronger than one. This is why we need each other. On our own we are likely to get frayed and torn apart by the challenges of life. One strand cannot bear the weight of life alone. But when we are twisted together into one with God and others, we become a cord that is not easily broken. Our combined strength makes each individual stronger.

Who are you bound together with and stronger because of the connection? In what areas of life could you use the strength of a three-strand rope so that you will not be quickly or easily broken?

CONNECTION CLUB

Live in harmony with one another.
Do not be proud, but be willing to associate
with people of low position. Do not be conceited.

(Romans 12:16)

CHRISTIANITY IS NOT A CLUB. There are some who might disagree with that statement, and there are some churches that may seem to resemble clubs from the outside. But at its core, following Jesus is not about belonging to something exclusive, but to something totally inclusive. Honestly, it's often easier to live alongside, connect with, and extend grace to people who are similar to us. But Jesus's love calls us to something much tougher.

Paul tells us we are to bless those who persecute us (see Romans 12:14–17). And Luke says, "Love your enemies, do good to those who hate you, bless those who curse you, pray for those who mistreat you" (Luke 6:27–28). Our verse for today instructs us not to be proud or conceited in our associations with others. That's a tough calling! But it's what connection in Christ is all about—loving and serving others, even those who are hard to love and serve. It doesn't mean that you shouldn't have close friends who agree with you on many things—people you can support and relate to. And it certainly doesn't mean that you should put yourself in abusive or dangerous situations to befriend others on your own. But if our circle of friends looks, believes, and acts just like we do, to the exclusion of the outcast, then we have missed a vital connection in Christ.

Who can you identify as someone who is hard to love, due to their issues or your own? Is there someone you have avoided due to your own pride? How can you reach out to that person in love this week?

SPURRED ON

And let us consider how we may spur one another on toward love and good deeds, not giving up meeting together, as some are in the habit of doing, but encouraging one another—and all the more as you see the Day approaching.

(Hebrews 10:24–25)

SPURS ARE A SYMBOL OF cowboys and the Wild West. But these metal tools are more than just a leftover from a glorified time gone by. Fitted onto the boots of the rider, spurs are used in many equestrian events to help the rider communicate with the horse, encouraging the horse to do exactly what the rider requires. Watch a bronco-riding event in a rodeo, and you'll see horse and rider come out of the gate. As soon as the horse starts kicking its rear legs into the air, the cowboy applies pressure high on the sides of the horse to encourage it to kick higher and faster, making for a more challenging ride and a higher score. It's where the phrase "spurring someone on" comes from.

In Hebrews, followers of Christ are told to "spur one another on"—not to kick higher and faster, but "toward love and good deeds." This kind of encouragement cannot be accomplished without connection. A cowboy on the side of the arena has no way to spur a horse. He has to be physically with the horse to make that connection. And we cannot spur one another on and encourage each other if we aren't connected. That's why the writer of Hebrews tells us not to give up meeting together. This kind of connection takes contact. Consistently meeting together allows us a connection that is not about gossip or fun or comfort or status, but about reminding one

another of our purpose in Christ and encouraging each other to action.

*Who in your life spurs you on? Who do you en-
courage? Do you need to recommit to meeting
together with other believers? What steps can
you take this week?*

BROKEN CONNECTIONS

For where two or three gather in my name,
there am I with them.

(Matthew 18:20)

THIS VERSE IS OFTEN USED to claim the presence of God with believers, whether gathered in a big or small group. And while it is true that we are not alone and that God is always with us, this verse in Matthew is more specific. Taken in context, it is about God's presence with us when the connection among believers is broken by sin and we are in need of restoration. The verses just before this one in Matthew 18 talk about dealing with sin in the church and what to do when a believer's sin impacts the unity of the body of Christ.

And so this verse is much more than just a vague assurance that God is with us wherever we go (because, in fact, He is with us even when we are alone and not only when we are with one or two others). It is a statement of God's desire to reconnect believers and restore us when sin breaks us apart. This passage in Matthew 18 gives instruction on how to deal with sin in a believer's life and expresses support for the decisions made by a group of believers together for the best of the community. God is with us. He is for us. And He wants to see every community of believers overcome the splintering power of sin.

Have you seen the separating power of sin? Why is it so important that restoration take place in a group of believers? How can God's promise to be with you help you to be part of that process?

Time for
COMPASSION

GOD'S COMPASSION

The LORD is gracious and compassionate,
slow to anger and rich in love.

(Psalm 145:8)

KIDS' MYSTERY BOOKS ARE FAMOUS for their tendency to do a classic bait-and-switch with main characters. You are introduced to a character who seems one way, but in the end you discover he is exactly the opposite: The smiling, tan boat driver turns out to be the diamond smuggler. But sometimes this happens in real life, too. We meet someone and form an opinion of them based on what we've seen or heard or due to a position the person has held. We make assumptions that shape our concept of that person. Sometimes initial impressions are right on, but other times they are turned on their head by further interaction.

Is our idea of God the same way? Perhaps things we've heard or experienced have caused us to think of God in a particular way. But when we search Scripture, talk with others, and reflect on our own lives, we realize the false assumptions we've made. Ever look at the world and feel that God is quick to anger and kind of stingy with His love? His true character couldn't be further from that—He is gracious, compassionate, slow to anger, and rich in love. What assumptions have you made? Are they accurate? Psalm 34:8 invites you to experience God's compassion and love for yourself and find out His true character: "Taste and see that the LORD is good."

What perceptions do you have of God? What perceptions have changed over time and with experience?

NOT OPTIONAL

He has shown you, O mortal, what is good.
And what does the LORD require of you? To act justly
and to love mercy and to walk humbly with your God.

(Micah 6:8)

DO YOU HAVE A JOB description? If you work in a typical setting, you probably have an official job description and tools to measure your performance. If you work at home or are a student, the requirements of your job may be less official but still there are expectations for what you must do and how to get it done. Job descriptions can be overwhelming and burdensome, but they can also bring freedom and clarity of expectations. If you know what is expected of you, it's easier to concentrate on meeting those requirements.

Micah 6:8 is a Christian's job description of sorts. And rather than being burdensome, it is designed to help us discover who we are in Christ and to help us fulfill His expectations for us. It tells us that our faith in God is all about compassion. We are "to act justly and to love mercy and to walk humbly with [our] God." These three things are summed up again when Jesus declares that the greatest commandment is to love God and the second is to love our neighbors (see Mark 12:30–31). Clearly, the nature of these commands isn't legalistic—they are a guide to help us define our purpose and then run after it as we also receive compassion from God.

*How do you measure up to this job descrip-
tion? Where can compassion increase in
your life?*

COMPASSION AND FORGIVENESS

Be kind and compassionate to one another, forgiving each other, just as in Christ God forgave you.

(Ephesians 4:32)

THE SMALL AND BEAUTIFUL AFRICAN country of Rwanda experienced something huge and ugly in 1994. The Rwandan genocide that took place left more than eight hundred thousand people dead. Many were killed by extremist militant groups, but many also died at the hands of their own neighbors who aligned with the ideals of the radical groups. The genocide left children without parents, parents without children, and many without the friends and neighbors they loved. Perpetrators were sent to jail, leaving even more women as widows to face the task of rebuilding their lives.

So how do you heal such pain? Forgiveness is the key. And the unlikely industry of coffee has been instrumental in bringing about opportunities for forgiveness and reconciliation. At coffee co-ops and washing stations built throughout communities, people have come and worked alongside their neighbors—the very people they must forgive. These places of community connection have taken forgiveness from an idealistic concept to a reality of everyday life. We can learn an important lesson from those in Rwanda about looking our enemy in the eye and learning to stand together in compassion and forgiveness.

What hurts have caused deep pain in your life? Who do you need to forgive? What steps can you take toward making that forgiveness a reality?

OPEN ARMS

*But while he was still a long way off,
his father saw him and was filled with
compassion for him; he ran to his son,
threw his arms around him and kissed him.*

(Luke 15:20)

THERE WAS A YOUNG MAN who took his inheritance, left his father's farm, and went to the city to live life his way. He squandered his money on fancy stuff and fast living. But after a while, he found himself alone, nowhere to turn. Sound familiar? It's the story of the Prodigal Son found in the Gospel of Luke.

Had the story ended there, it would be a depressing tale that has been lived out over and over again throughout history. But the story is transformed by a compassionate father. You see, when the young man hit rock bottom, he decided he would be better off as a servant in his father's house than feeding pigs. So he turned and went home. The picture of his return is beautiful. Luke tells us that "while he was still a long way off, his father saw him." The father was watching and waiting—not filled with anger but hopeful that his son would return. The father ran to his son, threw his arms around him, and kissed him. And later he clothed his son in the best robes and threw him a party. Why? Because the father loved him. Despite all the son's bad choices, the father was filled with compassion and love.

This is how our heavenly Father is toward us. When we go our own way and then turn back to Him, He is watching, waiting to throw His arms around us and welcome us back. We only have to turn and head home.

Do you believe God is waiting to welcome you with open arms? In what area of life do you need to turn and head home to God? Who do you need to open your arms of compassion to this week?

WEAR IT

*Therefore, as God's chosen people,
holy and dearly loved, clothe yourselves
with compassion, kindness, humility,
gentleness and patience.*

(Colossians 3:12)

DID YOU KNOW THERE ARE charity groups that provide spa services, makeovers, and new clothes for people in need? Volunteers donate their time and services to help people who suffer from cancer or medical issues, who have gone through hard times, or who have suffered abuse. The services provide not just a momentary escape for the individuals they serve but also help to boost self-esteem and motivation. Improving a person's outward appearance doesn't change his or her circumstances, but it does help one's mind-set.

We often focus on how the inward impacts the outward, but really the reverse is true as well. What is part of us on the outside also impacts the inside. Perhaps that is part of the reason Paul tells us in Colossians to "clothe" ourselves in "compassion, kindness, humility, gentleness and patience." We can't just hold these qualities inside; we have to wear them. And even when we don't feel particularly compassionate or kind, choosing to act outwardly according to these values helps them to become more a part of who we are on the inside.

It's a cycle: Outward impacts inward, which impacts outward. While we sometimes downplay the importance of clothing ourselves with the character traits we want to make an integral part of who we are, acting on them outwardly can jump-start our inner growth. So try them on for size and start the cycle moving. And as

Paul says later in the same chapter, "Whatever you do, whether in word or deed, do it all in the name of the Lord Jesus, giving thanks to God the Father through him" (verse 17).

What do your actions say about what is inside you? How can you start the cycle of inward change by choosing to act according to the traits you value?

A SIGN

*If anyone has material possessions
and sees a brother or sister in need
but has no pity on them, how can the love of
God be in that person?*

(1 John 3:17)

"HOMELESS AND HUNGRY. ANYTHING HELPS." Have you seen the signs? Most of us drive past them regularly. And while we know our response should be compassion, it is so easy to allow our compassion to be replaced with another "c" word: cynicism. And it's understandable—many of those who stand with signs take advantage of and abuse the generosity of others or use what they receive to further their cycle of poverty. So discernment and wisdom in how we give to others are good and necessary. But the question remains: When we encounter those in need—whether it is the homeless man on the corner, the widow next door, or the grocery clerk who is having a tough day—is our response one of compassion? It's a matter of the heart. Do we see needs and feel compassion, or do we experience a hardening of our hearts? Do we treat people in need with compassion, or do we do our best to ignore them?

What sign do the people around us see *us* holding? Our acts of compassionate love should be a sign to others that God's love lives in us. People should be able to read that message in our lives daily. In fact, John tells us in 1 John that when we don't have pity on those in need, the love of God is not in us. What is your sign saying to others today?

Does compassion flow from the love of God in you? Ask Him to help you see others through His eyes and have the courage to act in compassion.

COMPASSION FOR THE WEAK

*As a father has compassion on his children, so the L*ORD *has compassion on those who fear him; for he knows how we are formed, he remembers that we are dust.*

(Psalm 103:13–14)

THINK FOR A MINUTE OF all the animals you've ever felt compassion for—in a book, a movie, real life, or whenever. Your list is likely to include animals like bunnies, field mice, and songbirds. It might include elephants or other animals whose existence is threatened by exploitation. But your first response is not as likely to include more fierce animals like hyenas, water buffalo, or crocodiles. Why is that? Those animals may inspire us or scare us, but they rarely elicit compassion because we typically feel compassion for the weak. When we do feel compassion for the strong, it is often because of a weakness or a threat to their great strength.

In Psalm 103, David says that God has compassion on us because He knows we are weak. The all-powerful God knows that we were formed from the earth, that our lives are short, and that in death we will return to dust. He not only feels compassion for us, but He has acted on that compassion. He has made a way for things to be different. His compassion moved Him to send His own Son to die for our sins and give us eternal life. His compassion, acted out in love, saves us. This should not be discouraging to us, but rather inspiring. Through Christ, our lives have eternal significance and meaning, and we can live for a greater purpose. Just as He looks with compassion on us, we can look at others with His perspective. We can have compassion for others and offer them the same hope, grace, and connection He has given to us.

How does God's compassion inspire you to live with greater purpose? Who can you look at from God's perspective and share His compassion with today?

RUN HARD

*Therefore, since we are surrounded by such
a great cloud of witnesses, let us throw off everything
that hinders and the sin that so easily entangles.
And let us run with perseverance the race marked out
for us, fixing our eyes on Jesus, the pioneer
and perfecter of faith.*

(Hebrews 12:1–2)

HAVE YOU EVER WALKED THE racecourse after a run has ended? It's a mess! From start to finish the course is typically littered with all kinds of things: hats, shirts, coats, water cups, snack wrappers, and more. Why? Because as runners move through the course, they don't want to be weighed down by things they don't need. And with their eyes on the finish line and a crowd to cheer them on, runners often decide it's better to simply discard something rather than keep it with them.

It's a messy scene, but actually a challenging picture for the Christian life. Of course, we aren't encouraging reckless littering, but the idea that people are willing to drop the stuff that slows them down in order to accomplish their ultimate goal is inspiring. It's a picture of how we should be living and running after God, with our eyes so fixed on the finish line that we readily throw off things we don't need and things that slow us down or get in the way of our pursuing God. When we fix our eyes on Jesus and throw off the things that hold us back in our relationship with Him, we find ourselves getting closer to His goal for us. It may be actual physical things, or it may be habits, thoughts, relationships, or pain that entangles and slows us down. Freed from those things that hinder, we can grow in hope, grace, connection, and compassion as we run with perseverance.

It's race day—now is the time. Throw off what holds you back, join hands with others in the race, and run hard toward Jesus.

What slows you down and holds you back from your journey of faith with God? How can you begin to throw those things off as you run your race?

NOTES